MW01013040

Jazz Blues Styles

by Joe Diorio

Jazz Blues Solos in the Styles of Charlie Parker, Thelonius Monk, Sonny Rollins, and more.

Jazz Blues Styles is second in Joe Diorio s Right Brain Guitarist® series of books for jazz musicians. *Jazz Structures for the New Millennium* is the first. Visit www.joediorio.com for this and other Joe Diorio products.

ONLINE AUDIO

1	Solo 1: Sonny's Blues [:21]
2	Solo 2: Sonny's Syncopated Blues [:23]
3	Solo 3: Altered Chord Blues [:29]
4	Solo 4: Bird and Sonny Blues [:23]
5	Solo 5: Monk's Blues [:26]
6	Solo 6: The Bluesy Blues [:34]
7	Solo 7: Bird Blues [:26]
8	Solo 8: Parker's New Blues [:25]
9	Solo 9: Two Note Blues [:29]
10	Solo 10: Flat Five Blues [:29]

11	Solo 11: Octaves a la Wes Blues [:33]
12	Solo 12: Comping Blues [:33]
13	Solo 13: The Low Strings Blues [:22]
14	Solo 14: Accompany Yourself Blues [:30]
15	Solo 15: Walking Bass with Chords Blues [:33]
16	Solo 16: The Walking Bass Bird Blues [:34]
17	Blues Jam 1 in B♭ [2:56]
18	Blues Jam 2 in F [3:38]
19	Blues Jam 3 in G [3:14]
20	Blues Jam 4 in C [3:14]

All Rights Reserved in the U.S.A. and Internationally

Cover Design: Toby and Phyllis Weiss
Music copyist: Rick Schmunk
Editors: Narayani Diorio, Phyllis Weiss, Toby Weiss

The Right Brain
Guitarist® Series

To Access the Online Audio Go To:
www.melbay.com/99623MEB

Visit us on the Web at www.melbay.com — E-mail us at email@melbay.com

What You Can Learn from this Book

Within the context of the Blues, by studying this book you will learn:

- ◆ Styles of Jazz Blues

- ◆ Jazz ideas, phrases, and licks

- ◆ Jazz syncopation -- the rhythmic language of jazz

- ◆ Jazz phrasing -- the breath of jazz

- ◆ How to use the triplet, altered chords, and slash chords

- ◆ How to reharmonize the blues

- ◆ A new innovative vocabulary of jazz chord sequences

- ◆ How to use fragments of the chords to outline the harmony and create interesting new sounds

- ◆ How to play walking bass lines with chords

The Right Brain Guitarist ® Approach

The Right Brain Guitarist approach helps to direct your playing with your intuitive sense as opposed to your logical sense. While the left side of the brain is needed for our mechanical routine daily tasks and logical thinking, the right side of the brain is considered our artistic and intuitive side. It is from this side that many of our best and most creative ideas flow. It is the left side of the brain that often restricts our playing from rising to new heights. Its logical thinking can get in the way of creating fresh new ideas and soloing on new frontiers of creativity.

In the Right Brain Guitarist study guide section of this book, you will be reminded of approaches to use while studying and practicing music. We hope these ideas serve to expand your creative ability to come up with new, fresh, and inventive playing.

A compass keeps us always on the right track -- going in the direction we choose. Use the Right Brain Guitarist study guide as a compass while you practice the jazz blues music in this book. Always refer back to the Right Brain Guitarist concepts and incorporate them in your monthly practice regimen. This is how a compass works. We always refer back to it to make sure we are heading in the direction we choose. Choosing the direction of opening up to the intuitive and creative side of your brain is what the Right Brain Guitarist approach is all about.

Table of Contents

Introduction

Everybody wants to play the blues in some form or another. This book contains the blues from a jazz musician s point of view.

In the early 1950 s, the records of Charlie Parker, Sonny Rollins, Clifford Brown and Bud Powell dominated my record collection. My introduction to the blues was from their perspective. Blues as we know it had not reached the level of acceptance that it enjoys now. Some of the blues players of today were not even born, much less recorded in the 50 s.

So the blues for me comes from the jazz perspective. I have used quotes from the masters mingled with my own ideas to present jazz solos that will help anyone expand their jazz-blues vocabulary.

This book is replete with the devices that make jazz-blues different, i.e., syncopation, use of triplets, double time phrases, as well as a section dealing with jazz chords in the context of the blues progression. The lessons in this book will help you to evolve into a stronger player, whatever style you play.

Blues for all space cadets can be heard on two of my CDs: *Minor Elegance* with Robben Ford and on *Narayani*. One last point before you start: be sure to listen to the accompanying CD - this will help you hear the subtle nuances of the jazz-blues. It is just not possible to capture all these subtle nuances on the written page -- so be sure to use your ears and <u>listen</u>.
Also, when in doubt about the phrasing as shown on paper, listen to this CD and everything will clear up right away. Try to play along with me to become accurate.

We have added some trio tracks with Bob Magnusson on bass and Jim Plank on drums. This will provide an outlet for you to try the solos and have fun jamming. Listen a lot, for this is the magic secret... LISTEN.

Joe Diorio

Introduction to Solos

This section contains the solos that I play for you on the accompanying CD. In these solos, I ve used my own style and approaches to jazz blues as well as styles of other well known jazz musicians.

The Right Brain Guitarist®

Solo 1: Sonny's Blues

medium swing

Sonny s Blues was written with Sonny Rollins in mind. Every phrase flows into the next one with enough rhythmic variety to create a strong be-bop oriented solo. Listen to the CD to catch the subtle nuances in the phrasing. This is a good solo for creating variety in your blues playing.

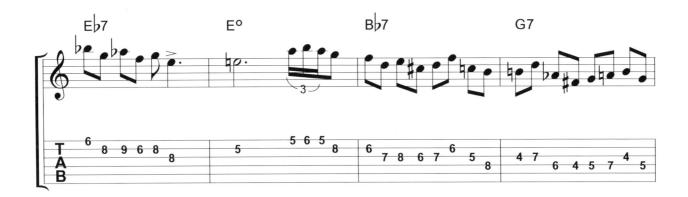

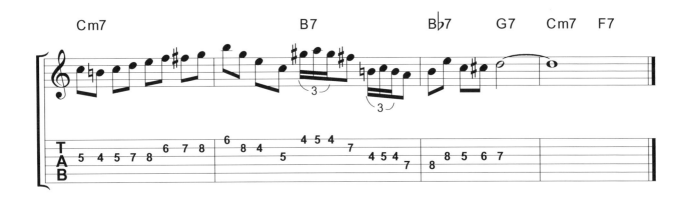

Solo 2: Sonny's syncopated blues

medium swing

This solo creates plenty of syncopation which gives it a push and pull feeling. Remember, the more melodic and rhythmic variety you create in a solo, the more interesting it is. This solo is ideal for learning this lesson.

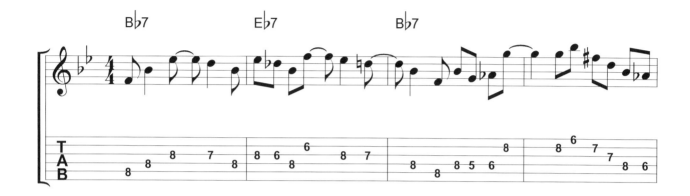

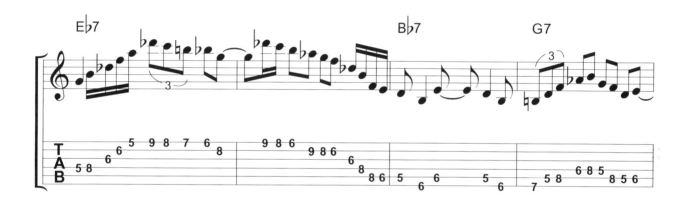

Solo 3: Altered chord blues

medium to fast

Here we are concentrating on altering the dominant chords. Notice how the first eight bars deal with dominant sharp eleven chords, while bars 8 and 10 deal with the dominant flat 9 chord. These harmonies appear quite frequently in jazz blues. Let your ear get used to them.

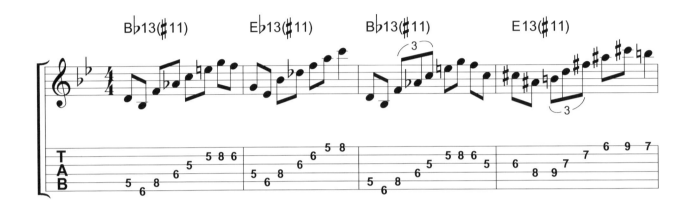

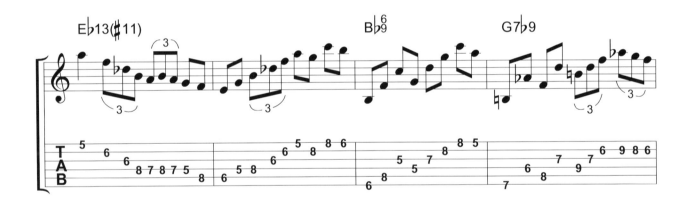

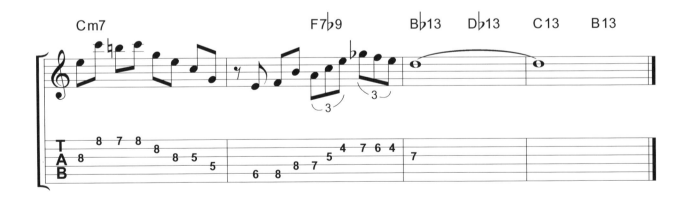

Solo 4: Bird and Sonny Blues

medium to fast

Note the use of the triplet in the last 3 solos. This is a common device used in jazz blues and will appear throughout this book, so learn it well. This solo is bop oriented, get as much of this style into your playing as possible. It is a great foundation for all styles of improvising.

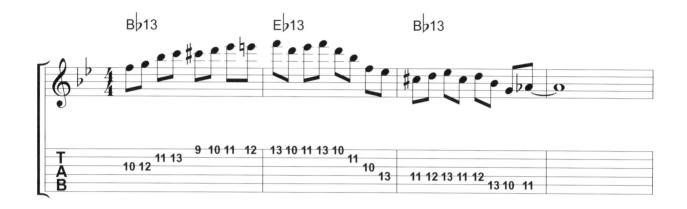

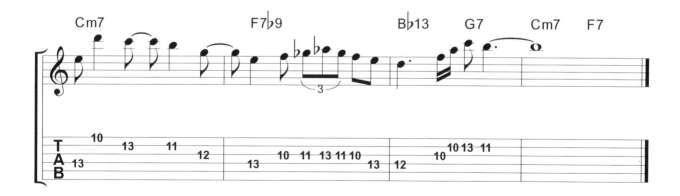

Solo 5: Monk's Blues

medium walking tempo

By using the minor second interval on top and outlining the chord with the root bass note we have an imitation of Thelonious Monk s music. If it is too hard to hold down the bass note, strike it first, release it and grab the top part of the chord. I use this type of voicing for comping behind someone, but be careful to mix it with other chords. Overdoing the seconds can be boring.

Solo 6: The Bluesy Blues

slow funky tempo

This is the closest to pure blues in this book. The triplet is the outstanding rhythm.

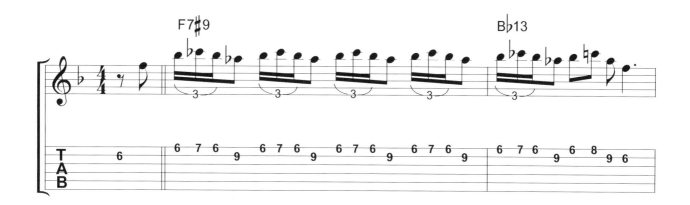

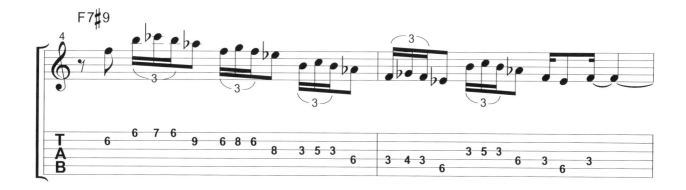

Solo 6: The Bluesy Blues (cont.)

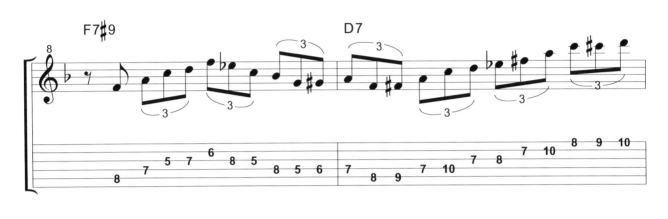

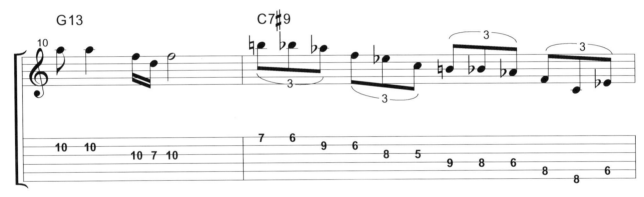

Solo 7: Bird Blues

medium to fast

In keeping with introducing as many pure jazz ideas as possible, this solo is Charlie Parker flavored.

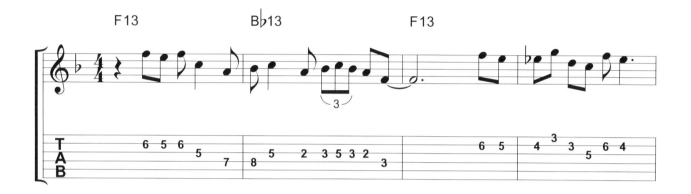

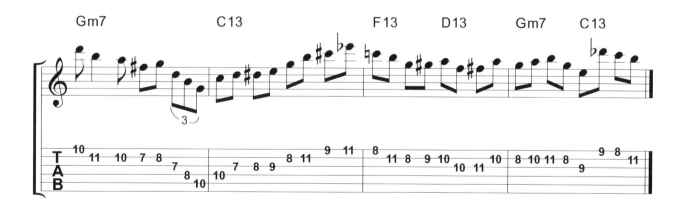

Solo 8: Parker's New Blues

medium tempo

This progression was introduced by Charlie Parker in the 1950 s. It is sometimes referred to as the *Blues for Alice* progression. Any real book will have this tune among its collection. At first it may challenge you, but when it is mastered it is great fun. The solo also has a be-bop orientation.

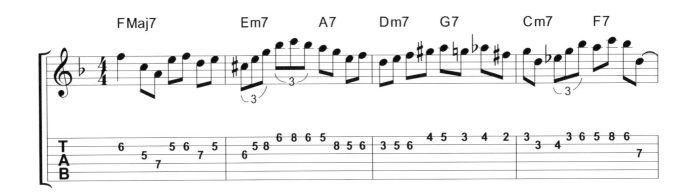

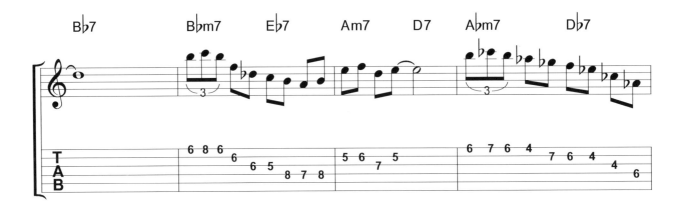

Solo 9: Two Note Blues

medium relaxed… not too fast

Here we introduce fragments of the chord to outline the harmony. Several top guitarists use this approach at times along with other harmonic devices from their arsenal of great chords. You will notice that if you put the fragments together they form a chord shape. We are taking a chord we like and breaking it into pieces. Try this with the other chords you know.

Solo 10: Flat Five Blues

walking tempo… not too fast

This solo outlines the dominant flat five sound through the use of chord shapes. Since this sound is used in so many harmonic situations, the blues is a good way to become accustomed to it. Notice if you play two notes at a time you are creating fragments as described in solo 9.

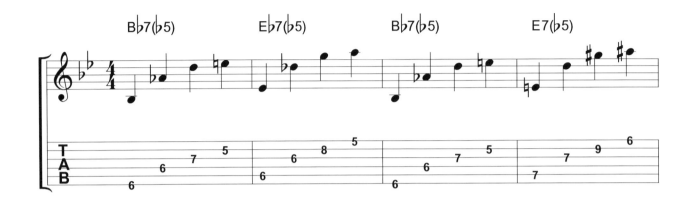

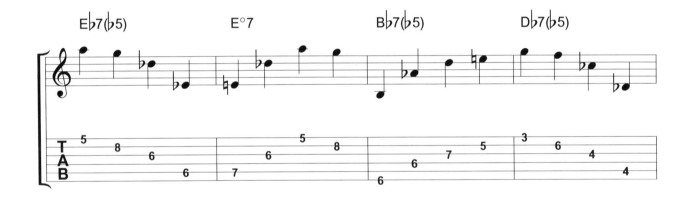

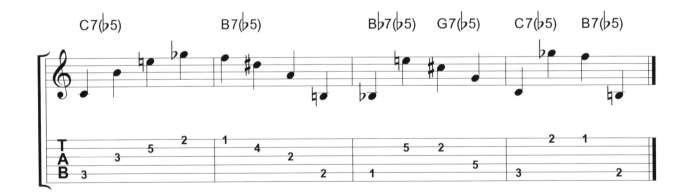

Solo 11: Octaves a la Wes Blues

slow to medium feel

We are imitating the master Wes Montgomery s octave technique. Find the fingerings that are comfortable for you and just play.

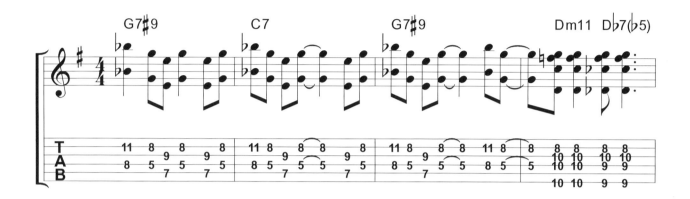

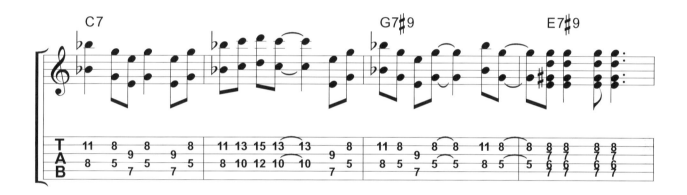

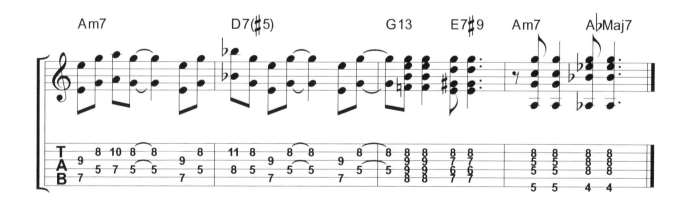

Solo 12: Comping Blues

medium tempo

The comping blues employs fragments along with little nudges to push everything straight ahead. These two-note compositions will do wonders for your hands and head, they will start you to think in terms of intervals as opposed to grips or shapes. Be sure to note the relationship between the two notes and the harmony it outlines.

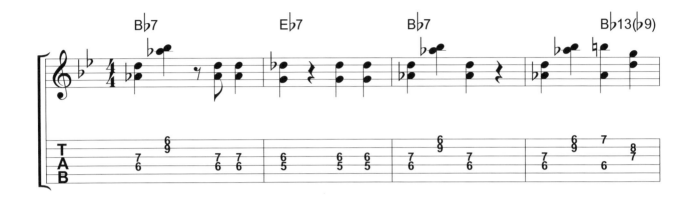

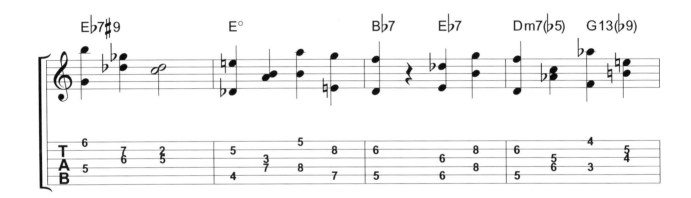

Solo 13: The Low Strings Blues

medium to fast

It s great to play on the low strings as it gives a sort of growl. Try to improvise and transpose your favorite licks and the ideas from this book to the low register.

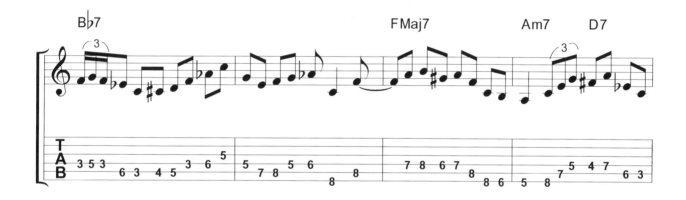

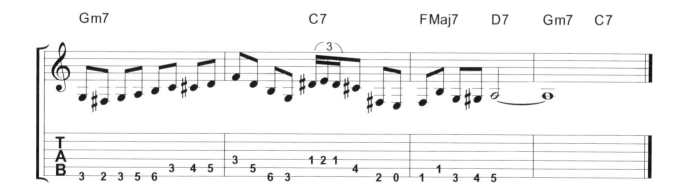

Solo 14: Accompany Yourself Blues

medium blues feel

Back yourself up with parts of the chords when you are soloing. This is a very effective device, using rhythmic figures with a simple melody line. Simple, but strong.

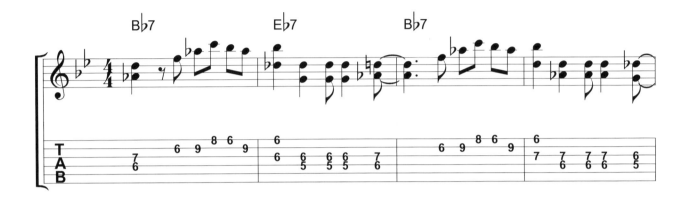

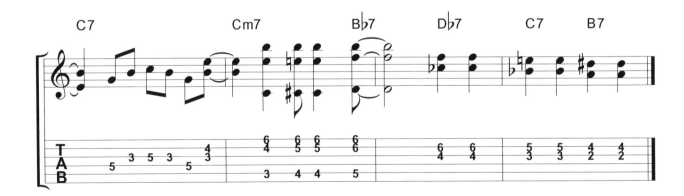

Solo 15: Walking Bass with Chords Blues

medium... not too fast

Play this one slowly at first. You need to get all the fingering correct and comfortable, then increase to a good walking tempo. Keep the bass notes strong, then take some liberties. Be creative, leave out some notes or add some.

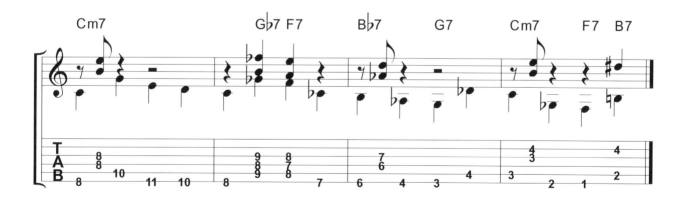

Solo 16: The Walking Bass Bird Blues

medium tempo

The *Blues for Alice* progression is used here incorporating tenths to enforce parts of the bass line. Tenths add a strong feel to the bottom note and is another way to play bass lines. Once again, when creating this type of solo, keep it simple.

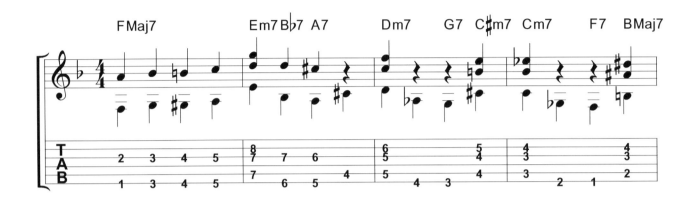

Blues for All Space Cadets

Pay close attention to the unison notes. They are to be played on separate strings. This composition stretches the blues form, but when played up tempo, you can feel the pulse of the blues.

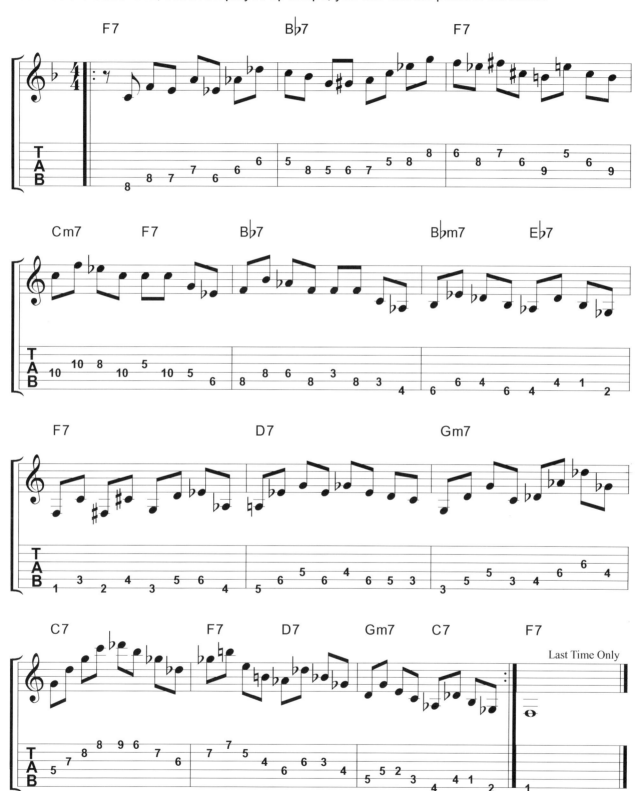

Chord Examples and Pr ogressions

In this section of the book I introduce 12 chord progressions and 16 chord examples. In these examples you will find the most simple chord to the most complex in different juxtapositions. This was done to introduce many ways of playing the blues harmonically. The benefits are far reaching as these chords can be used in other situations besides the blues.

Some are easy to hear and others sound more advanced. Be patient and give them all a chance to sink in. The challenge will help all areas of your playing.

If a chord is too much of a stretch for your hand, reduce the amount of a notes to a few. This will help, as a chord need not have every note in it to be effective. If at first a chord sounds strange to you this week, wait because it may sound good next week -- for our ears are always growing. I would highly recommend that you get used to the slash chords, they are so much a part of contemporary harmony. There are many great altered chords in all qualities as well as some cluster harmonies.

If you just study the chord section your harmonic ability will be greatly enhanced. A great musician once told me Harmony is infinite. Meditate on that for awhile. Go slowly and don t rush.

Blues Progressions

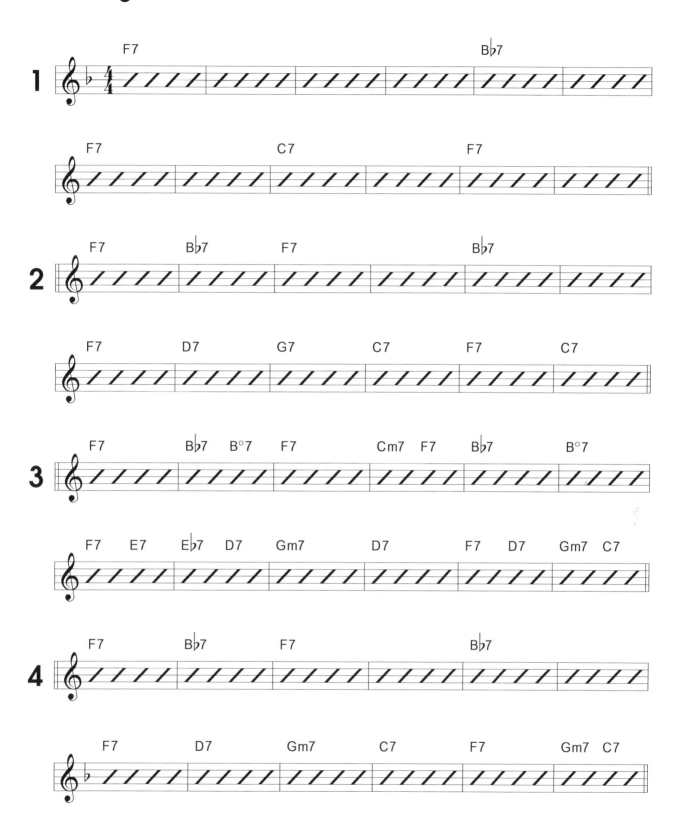

Blues Progressions (cont.)

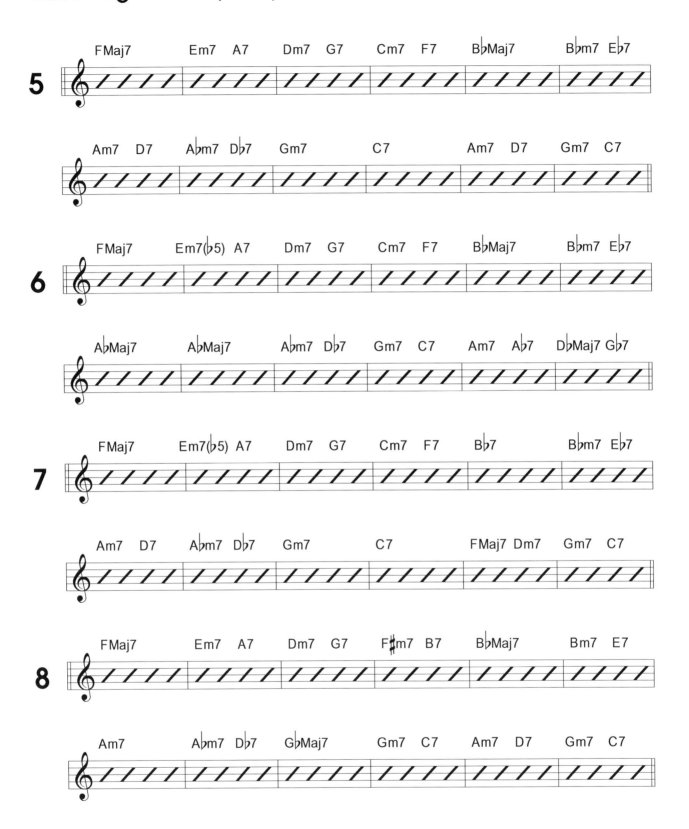

5

| FMaj7 | Em7 A7 | Dm7 G7 | Cm7 F7 | B♭Maj7 | B♭m7 E♭7 |

| Am7 D7 | A♭m7 D♭7 | Gm7 | C7 | Am7 D7 | Gm7 C7 |

6

| FMaj7 | Em7(♭5) A7 | Dm7 G7 | Cm7 F7 | B♭Maj7 | B♭m7 E♭7 |

| A♭Maj7 | A♭Maj7 | A♭m7 D♭7 | Gm7 C7 | Am7 A♭7 | D♭Maj7 G♭7 |

7

| FMaj7 | Em7(♭5) A7 | Dm7 G7 | Cm7 F7 | B♭7 | B♭m7 E♭7 |

| Am7 D7 | A♭m7 D♭7 | Gm7 | C7 | FMaj7 Dm7 | Gm7 C7 |

8

| FMaj7 | Em7 A7 | Dm7 G7 | F♯m7 B7 | B♭Maj7 | Bm7 E7 |

| Am7 | A♭m7 D♭7 | G♭Maj7 | Gm7 C7 | Am7 D7 | Gm7 C7 |

26

Blues Progressions (cont.)

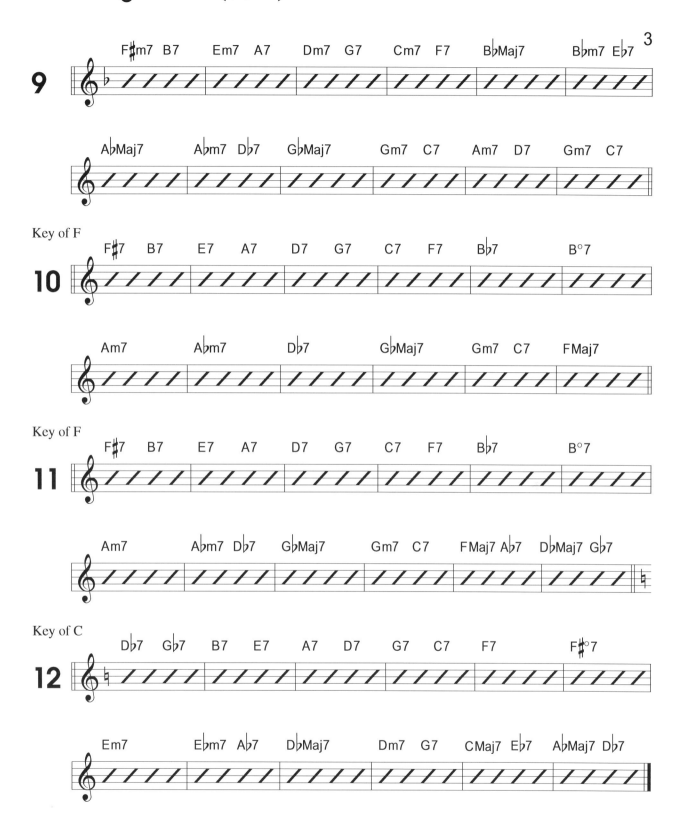

Chord Example 1

Thirds and sevenths are the simplest way to outline the harmony. You can get a great blues feel with these two notes.

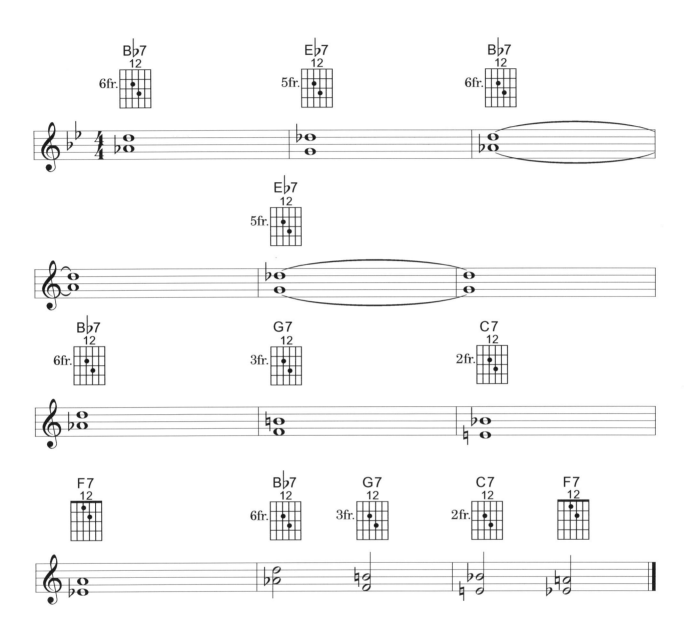

Chord Example 2

Examples 2 and 3 are common jazz chords. The top note of the chord is following a melodic line for better voice leading. Always try to lead your chord melodically instead of just grabbing any chord shape.

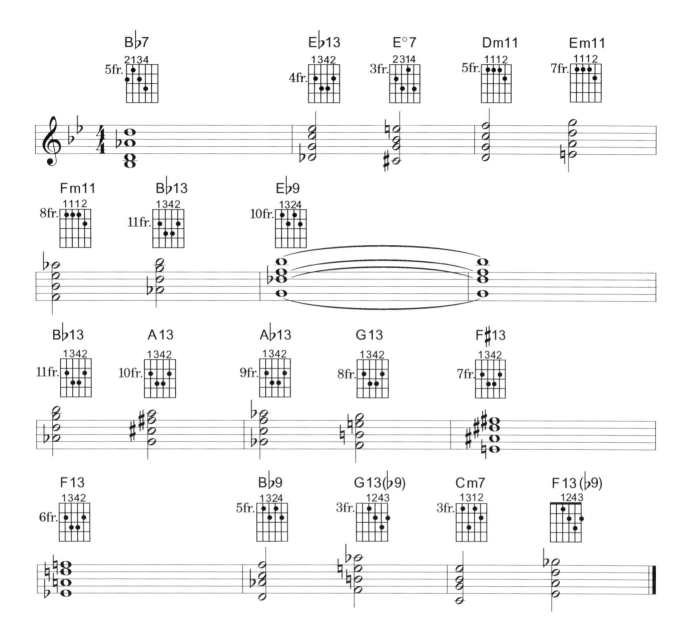

Chord Example 3

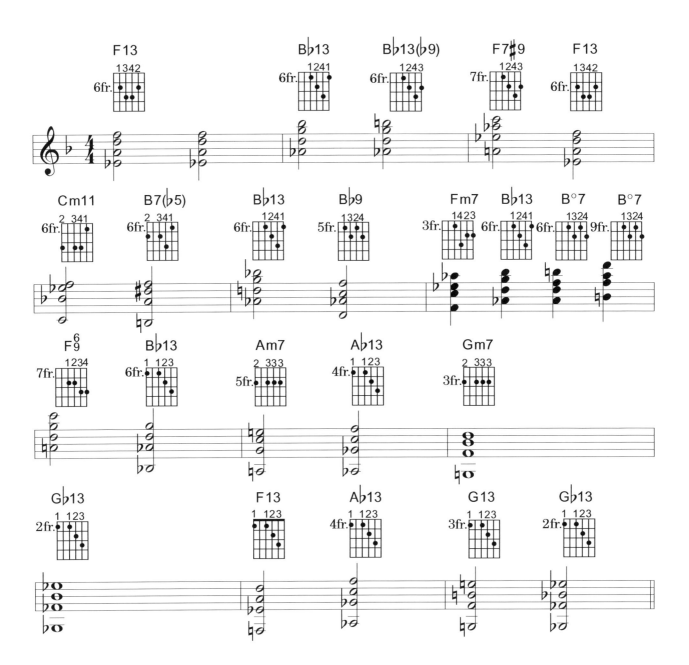

Chord Example 4

Examples 4 and 5 are the Charlie Parker *Blues for Alice* progression. Example 4 chords are quite useful because the chords are easy to hear and play.

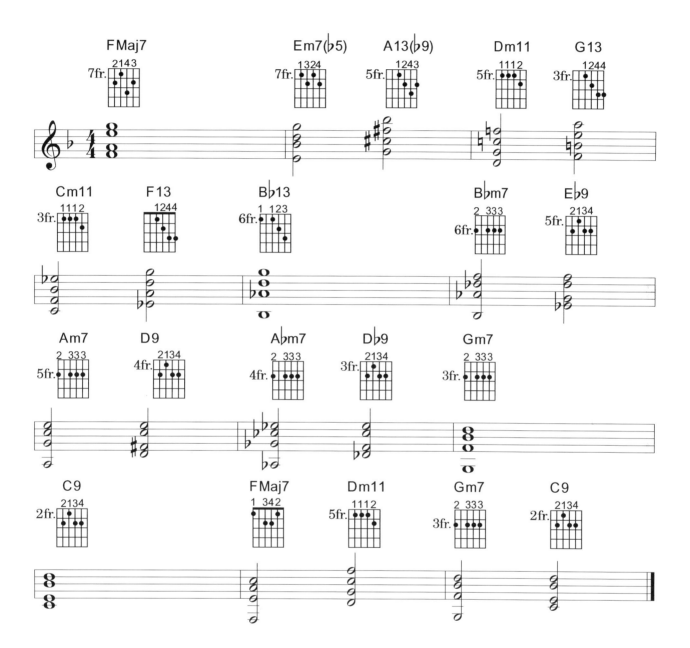

Chord Example 5

Example 5 is the same progression stretching the harmonic sound. New voicings, unusual stretches, beautiful two-five-ones are introduced for use elsewhere.

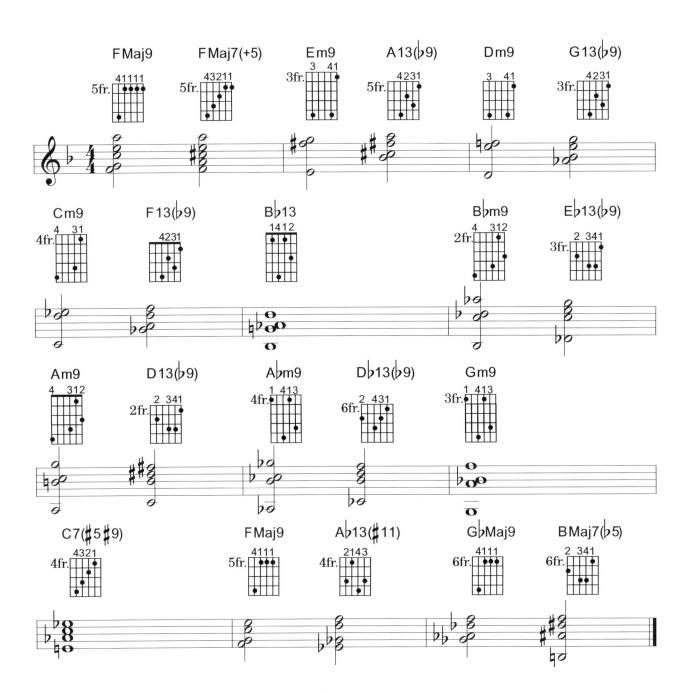

Chord Example 6

More new chords and some slash chords. Remember this is still a blues. Notice how many triads are hidden within these chords. Take any triad and place any bass note below and see how many new slash chords you can create.

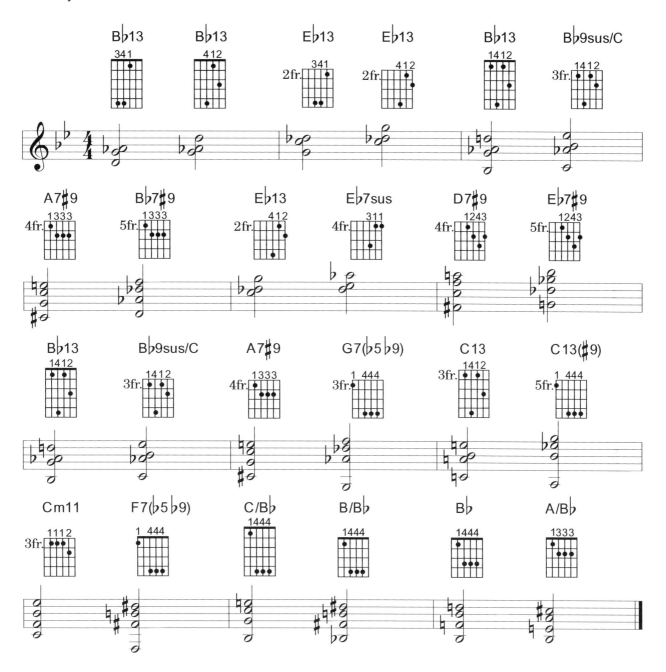

Chord Example 7

By keeping the note Bflat on top and moving the chords underneath, we create a top note pedal effect. The chords are not hard but the results are fresh.

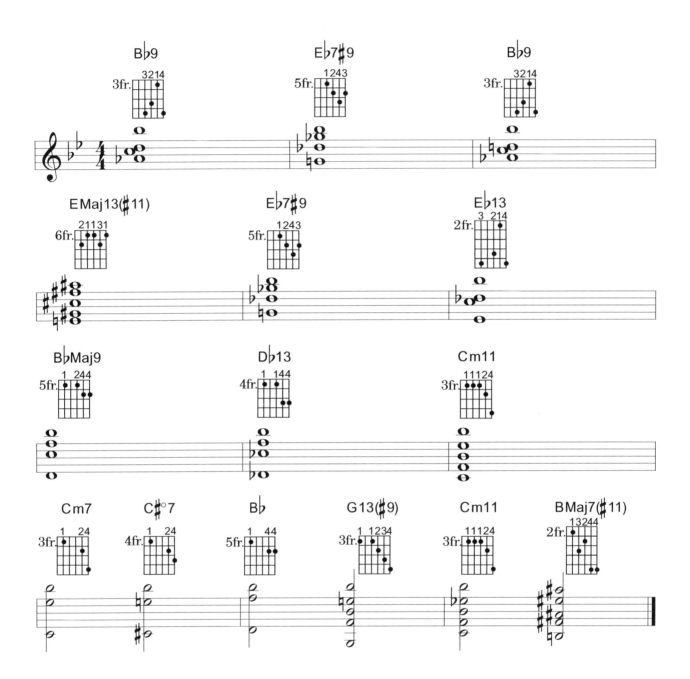

Chord Example 8

This example shows one chord a beat with a melody line on the top. No unusual chords but the effect is melodic.

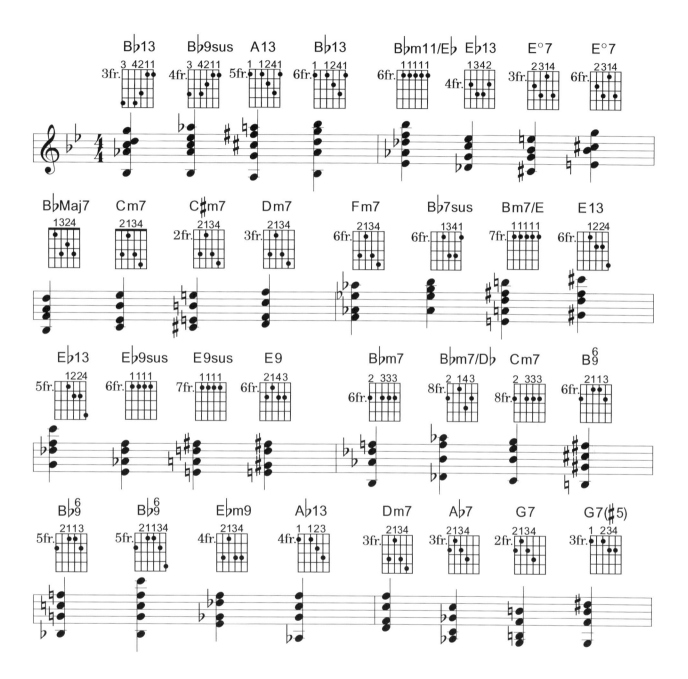

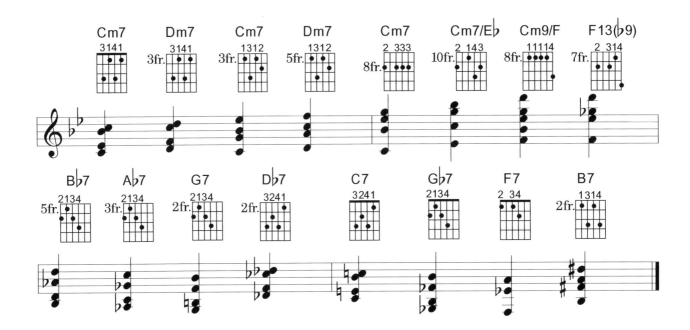

Chord Example 9

Note the use of 3 note voicings in bars 1-2, 5-7-8. With the use of minor seconds on top of the chord the sound is quite nice, especially when used with other type voicings. Also notice the unusual G7 altered at bar 8 and F7 altered at bar 10.

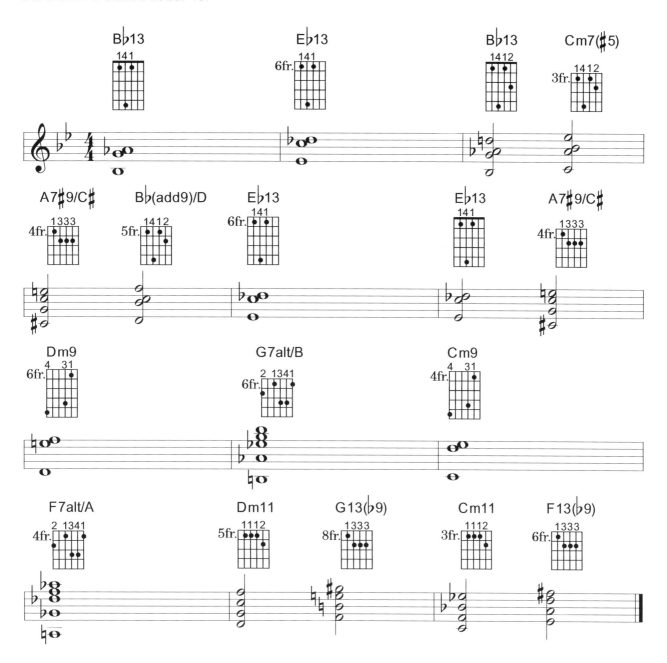

Chord Example 10

These are the voicings used for Monk s Blues (solo 5). We use minor seconds on top with the root of the chord in the bass.

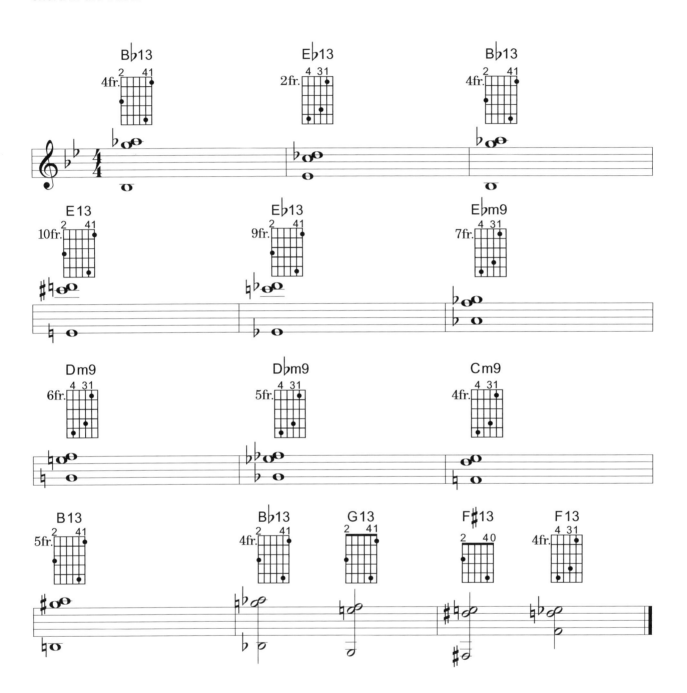

Chord Example 11

This example stretches us pretty far. Once again notice all the triads buried in these chords. Don t let the symbols worry you, listen to the sound of the chord. Try using some of these chords in the tunes that you already play. Note the 3 new sus. chords in bars 1 and 2. Plenty of altered dominants also.

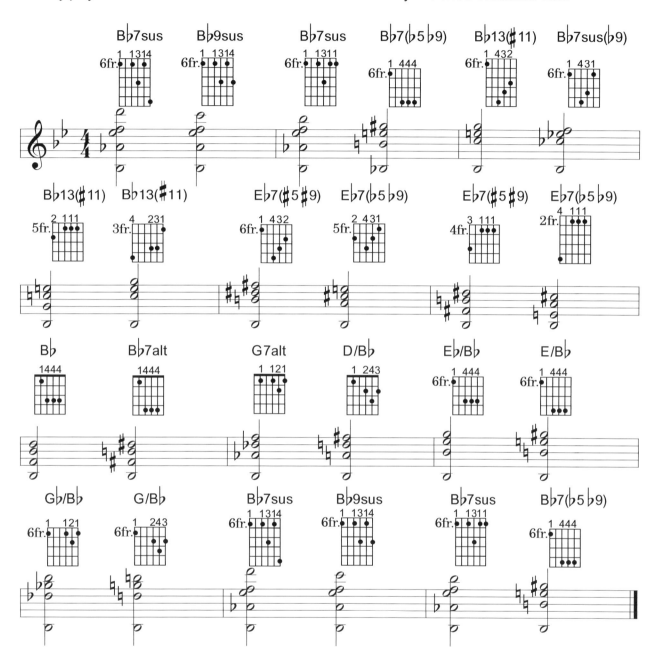

Chord Example 12

With all the slash chords you are probably wondering, Is this still the blues? Well, maybe not the way we are used to hearing it. When it gets too far out, write the basic blues chord progression on top of the bars to establish a point of reference. This way you can see and hear the working of the slash chords.

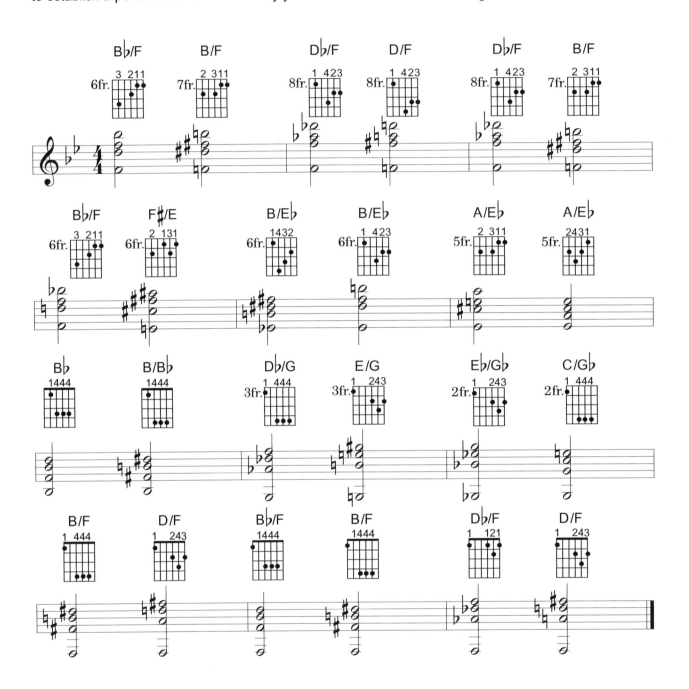

Chord Example 13

Bar one through seven are cluster chords. These chords usually have seconds involved which is part of the case here. The sound is very tight and the stretch is difficult, but for those with a good stretch they are useful. Note the slash in the last two bars outlining the turnaround. Bflat seventh altered, G seventh altered, C seventh altered, B seventh altered -- a good use of slash chord harmony.

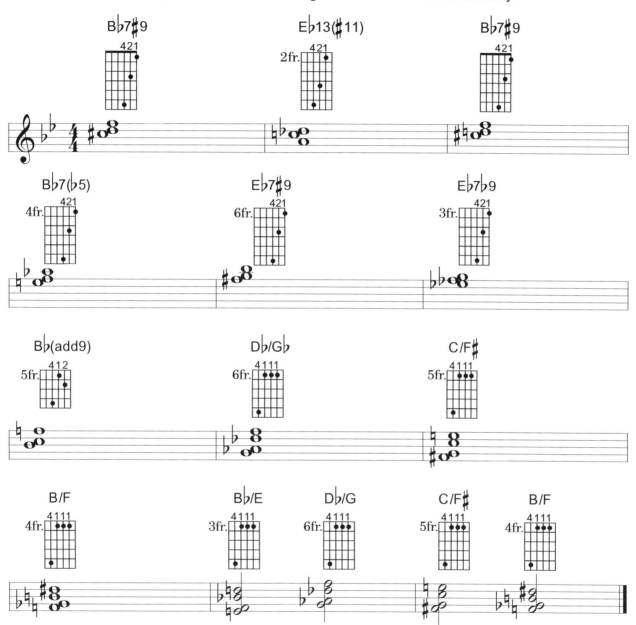

Chord Example 14

Look at blues progression number 12 on page 27 and you will see that it is the foundation for chord examples 14, 15, and 16. These three examples are in the key of C major. They start on the flat two in C major, i.e. D flat, and using dominant seventh chords, progresses two beats each through the cycle of fourths, to the 5th bar. I have altered all the dominant chords in example 14.

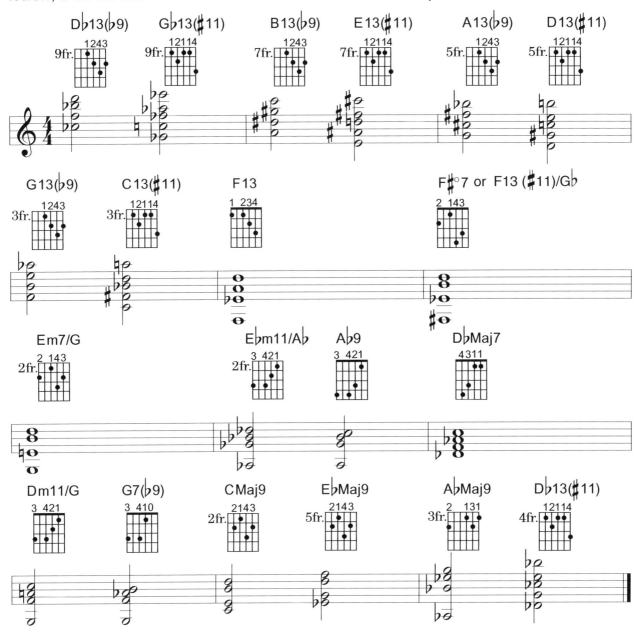

Chord Example 15

Here some additional chords are added to the original progression. With the use of minor seventh and minor ninth chords in the first four bars, the tension is less.

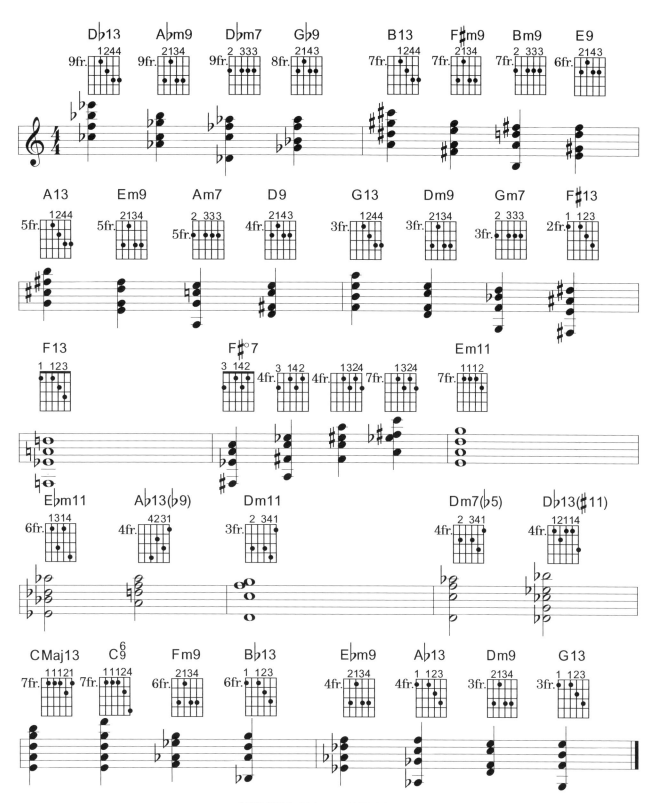

Chord Example 16

This makes use of slash chords to outline the altered dominant in the first 4 bars. This is not a common every day blues progression, but I include it because it presents a challenge. All these dominant chords can be used to heighten the tension from time to time while playing a simpler blues progression. Go forward and don t stop until the goal is reached!

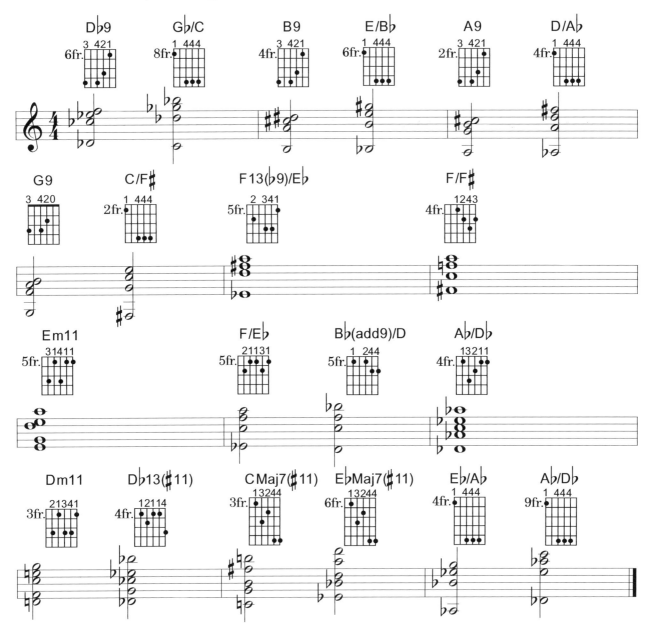

Right Brain Guitarist ® Study Guide

Cultivating a Creative Environment

This concept deals with issues pertaining to music but will offer different ways to approach it. The ideas presented here will elevate us to more creative heights and give us a clearer insight into the depths of music. The process is enigmatic. Sometimes it works fast and at other times slow. Which ever pertains to you, please be patient.

Find a place that you call your own, even if it s a small corner, if possible, with incoming light. Try to avoid darkness. Keep it neat, clutter and noise free. By going to your creative place each day you bombard that area with your music and your creative powers. Try doing the same with your inner self.

Find a place within your self that s happy, peaceful, quiet, and creative. Go there often to contemplate your music, your life, and your creativity. The deeper you go inside the music and yourself, the more profound your musical statement.

Have photos of your heroes around your private place. This will be a constant reminder to you of what can be accomplished. When I look at my photos I find inspiration to go higher in my music. In my room I have photos of Bird, Trane, Wes, Ravi Shankar, Picasso and others.

When you sit down in your space, be quite for a few moments. Ask the creative source what it is you should work on. Usually this comes as a fast intuitive flash, go with it. Release the tensions from your body. Stop the mind from racing. Realize the creative source is there to help you. Be grateful for what has come to you. Surrender yourself to the music.

Don t try to control the situation. Relax and let go. If for some reason you feel a block, go to that place and see yourself releasing it. Try a short affirmation like: I am now in touch with my higher creative source or I am a channel for creative energy.

Each person knows when it s time to stop. When that happens give thanks to your Muse and sit for a few minutes contemplating what took place. Sometimes there is more that wants to come through; it s like a bonus.

These ideas have been around for a while. I think it s time we, as musicians, incorporate them into our life style. Go forward.

Gesture Improvising
Gesture Improvising is tapping into the right side of the brain. It is avoiding the areas where you are already comfortable and using the instinctive and intuitive side of your mind. This exercise will bring to the surface new creative ideas. In my video, Creative Jazz Guitar I demonstrate Gesture Improvising. This right brain area is where you will find your new and creative ideas.

How to Gesture Improvise:
1. Start by playing quarter notes, be sure that you do not start in a position you re used to. Relax your fingers and start to play all over your instrument, letting your fingers guide you. Don t worry how it sounds, this is creating at a basic level. At some point switch to 8th notes, this speeds up the process. Do the same thing again with 16th notes. Try this exercise slowly for about 5 to 10 minutes. Take a break and repeat the process.

2. Next, repeat the previous exercise but listen closely to what notes your fingers are playing. Can you recognize them? If not, don t worry, in time you will. At this point you are developing your instinct to create momentum and hear what you are playing.

3. Now, pick a simple Blues or a tune you know well enough so you don t have to think about it. Keep the harmony somewhere in the back of your mind and begin to Gesture Improvise a tune or Blues all over the instrument. Do not play what you already know. Stretch for something new, relax and improvise. If possible, record your session to monitor your progress. Are you having fun yet? Do this exercise often, 10 to 15 minutes at a time. Don t tire yourself out, which means you re thinking too much.

4. Next, without your guitar, visualize and hear a single solo in your head. Immediately try to recreate what you heard. If it comes out differently, build upon whatever came through. Remember not to burden yourself with a lot of rules. We are creating! Give yourself permission to be creative. Hearing solos in your head should be an on going process —— no matter what you re doing, try timing yourself and sing in your head a 5 minute solo. Did it feel loose and creative? Try again and again; let it be part of your musical life style.

5. At this point, let s add rhythmical figures to all the above exercises. At first try one you know well and use it a lot. From time to time add new ones. Listen to all instruments for new ideas.

This is as far as we should go with these exercises for now. I will elaborate further in future columns.

Practicing Without the Instrument
This approach to mental practice will improve your ear, memory, and technique. First, let us start real easy by visualizing a simple piece you are *very* familiar with i.e. Happy Birthday or Jingle Bells. Can you see the notes in your head? If not, look at the music, memorize it, and then go back and visualize the simple piece. Now see all the intervals in your head and sing the song. This will help you to hear intervals and see them at the same time.

Next, try working with scale patterns; at first slowly and gradually increasing your speed. This whole approach builds your mental technique which will directly help build your physical technique. Practice every day for a while on music you are already familiar with scales, arpeggios, chord progressions, tunes, etc.

Last, apply this approach to your own solos. See and hear them in your head first before you play them. Only practice will get you there. So start now. If you don t know your intervals, now is the time to learn them.

Take a Risk a Day
There may be areas on your instrument that seem like foreign countries to you. You may have no clue as to what is going on there. Your first risk is to investigate them.

RISK 1. What about the bottom strings? Can you play a complete solo on them? Do you know your chord voicings on the bottom four strings i.e. triads and 7th chords, strings E, A, D, G or strings 6, 5, 4, 3? Take a bold risk and start playing things you already know in these areas. Can you play the melody there? Can you comp there?

RISK 2. Playing in a new key. Start by playing a tune you already know a half a step away from the original. Everything may go blank for a minute, but after you get oriented, you ve just learned something new. Now transpose to new keys in new areas.

RISK 3. Play through the cycle of 4th s. Cycle through with just major 7th chords. i.e. C major7 to F major7 to B flat major, E flat major, A flat major, etc., until you return to C major7. Make up melodies as you cycle. Try the same with dominant 7th chords: C7, F7, B flat7, etc. And altered dominants, i.e. C7 flat 5, F7 flat 5, B flat 7 flat 5, etc. Now try II V 1 cycles in major and minor. Major: Dmi7, G7, CMa7, Gmi7, C7, FMa7 etc. Minor: Dmi7 flat5, G7 flat9, Cmi6. Gmi7 flat5, C7 flat9, Fmi6, etc.

These ideas for risk-taking will help you to get started. Whatever areas of playing you have been avoiding in your practice regimen, that is the place to take a risk. Let this become a habit. It will pay great musical dividends.

Keeping Yourself Inspired Seven Days a Week
Each day of the week choose one subject and work on it all day long. Pick your weak areas. A typical week might look something like this:

Monday: Gesture improvising, all day. Letting go, feeling your way up and down the neck, checking out the possibilities. This usually starts out being abstract and works its way into more melodic playing. Plus the bonus of creating new ideas for future use. Maybe a new melody or a new chord progression. Here the basic idea is to shut off the thinking process and let your fingers and your feeling or intuition take over. Doing this all day gives us plenty of time to really get the idea of the exercise.

Tuesday: Melodic playing. Today we start to put two or more notes together that sound pretty . Take a look at your REAL BOOK and notice how some of the great tunes are made up of simple intervals. Some of them are short scale passages. This gives us a clue that it does not take much to write or play a good melody. Approach this exercise like the gesture improvising, i.e. playing any two notes until you find something that sounds decent, then begin to add to it with other melodic sounding intervals. Write at least one tune this day, and it will help you to think melodically and will add more substance to any style.

Wednesday: New chords. In the beginning there were fingers, and those fingers were meant to move. This is the objective today, to take any chord you know and move one finger at a time up and down the neck as far as you can reach. This is possibly the most simple way of finding new chords. Every time you move a finger you create a new chord. Some sound great and others don t sound so great. Start with a simple G7, 7th, 3rd, 5th, i.e. G, F, B, D. (6,4,3,2, strings) in the 3rd position. Example: move D to D sharp. This is G7 with a sharp 5. Move to E natural. This is G13. Move to F. This is G7. This is the process on all strings ascending and descending. After this is completed try moving two notes. This is being creative. Experiment.

Thursday: New melodies and new chords. This day we take some of the melodies created on Tuesday and add some of the new-found chords from Wednesday and put them together. Don t judge your new pieces but keep trying until you find something you like. Remember you have all day to come up with something that makes you feel good. If you write two bars you are a big winner. Also, try to take the new chords and use them in some of the tunes you know. Or make up your own progressions with them. You are being creative this day.

Friday: Listen to music all day long, new and old CDs. Get saturated and make notes of the players style, how they phrase, keep time, how they let space and silence become part of their solos. Can you recognize sounds and influences? Can you remember a few ideas that you can play? Are they available for a lesson? Be eclectic! Listen to rock, jazz, classical, world music, anything. Be inspired this day.

Saturday: What caught your musical fancy? Was there something this week that made you light up? This is the day to investigate further and go deeper into that subject. Try to understand what moves you. Is there a possible direction for you to take? If it caught your fancy, stick with it until it reveals itself to you. This day may change your life!

Sunday: Repose, silence, and meditation. Be still this day and listen for the inner voice to guide you. Ask your guide questions and be ready for the answers. Trust and they will come. Remember, your intuition is your very best friend. Listen to it and be ready to act on it. Be still, be quiet, and be ready.

Arrange your seven days your own way. Add subjects that you love. Add new directions from time to time. Go slowly, enjoy the journey and grow.

Other Books and CDs by Joe Diorio

¥ *Stateside* -- Joe Diorio, Bob Magnussion, Jim Plank form a magnificant trio on this CD of classic American standards. Diorio Jazz Records.

¥ *Jazz Play Along CDs* -- Joe Diorio, Bob Magnusson, and Jim Plank. With standards such as *Just Friends, Blue Bossa, Autumn Leaves, All the Things You Are*, and more! Diorio Jazz Records

¥ *20th Century Impressions* with Jeff Berlin on bass and Vinnie Colaiuta on drums. Diorio Jazz Records $16.95

¥ *I Remember You* a tribute to Wes Montgomery with Steve Bagby on drums and Steve LaSpina on bass. RAM Records $16.95

¥ *Jazz Structures for the New Millennium* a vocabulary of modern intervallic jazz ideas for jazz musicians. Includes a CD with all examples played by Joe. JoeDiorio.com $24.95

¥ *Giant Steps* an in-depth study of John Coltranes classic. An instructional book for jazz musicians. Includes a CD. Warner Brothers Publications $19.95

¥ *Creative Jazz Guitar* -- Explore Joes concepts of playing from the right side of the brain. Unleash your creativity with this unique and informative video lesson. VHS video in NSTC and PAL formats. $49.95

¥ *Fusion Guitar* -- Straight-Ahead and contemporary guitar solos based on classic jazz progressions. $17.95

Place your order in Joe Dioro's on-line market place at
www.joediorio.com

I hope you enjoy studying the subject of jazz-blues with me. I wish you peace. Go forward.

Joe Diorio, September 2000

35064457R00028